First Facts™

The Senses

Tasting

by Rebecca Olien

Consultant:
Eric H. Chudler, PhD, Research Associate Professor
Department of Anesthesiology, University of Washington
Seattle, Washington

Capstone
press
Mankato, Minnesota

First Facts is published by Capstone Press,
151 Good Counsel Drive, P.O. Box 669, Mankato, Minnesota 56002.
www.capstonepress.com

Library of Congress Cataloging-in-Publication Data
Olien, Rebecca.
  Tasting / by Rebecca Olien.
  p. cm. —(First facts. The senses)
  Summary: "Explains the sense of taste and how the tongue works as a sense
organ"—Provided by publisher.
  Includes bibliographical references and index.
  ISBN 0-7368-4304-3 (hardcover)
  1. Taste—Juvenile literature. I. Title. II. Series.
QP456.O45 2006
612.8'7—dc22   2004027224

Editorial Credits
Wendy Dieker, editor; Juliette Peters, designer; Molly Nei, illustrator;
  Kelly Garvin, photo researcher/photo editor

Photo Credits
Capstone Press/Karon Dubke, cover, 6–7, 10 (all), 12–13, 16–17, 21
Corbis/Jose Luis Pelaez Inc., 14; Tom Brakefield, 20
Getty Images Inc./Camille Tokerud, 1; Ryan McVay, 15; Sandy King, 5
Pete Carmichael, 19
Photodisc, 12–13 (background)

1 2 3 4 5 6 10 09 08 07 06 05

Table of Contents

The Sense of Taste

People tell foods apart by different tastes. The sense of taste lets us know what is good to eat. **Taste buds** in the tongue and mouth send messages to the brain. People **crave** foods their bodies need. Spoiled foods taste bad.

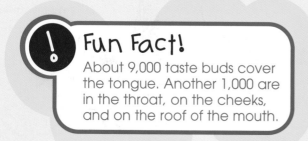

Fun Fact!
About 9,000 taste buds cover the tongue. Another 1,000 are in the throat, on the cheeks, and on the roof of the mouth.

How Saliva Works

The **saliva** in your mouth works to help you taste food. Saliva breaks food down into tiny bits. The tiny bits soak into your taste buds. Without saliva, you couldn't taste foods.

! Fun Fact!
In one year, a person makes enough saliva to fill two bathtubs.

The Tongue

The tongue is covered with bumps. Taste buds are inside the bumps. Food soaks into the taste buds.

Each taste bud has taste **sensors**. The sensors send taste messages to your brain through **nerves**. Your brain tells you how food tastes.

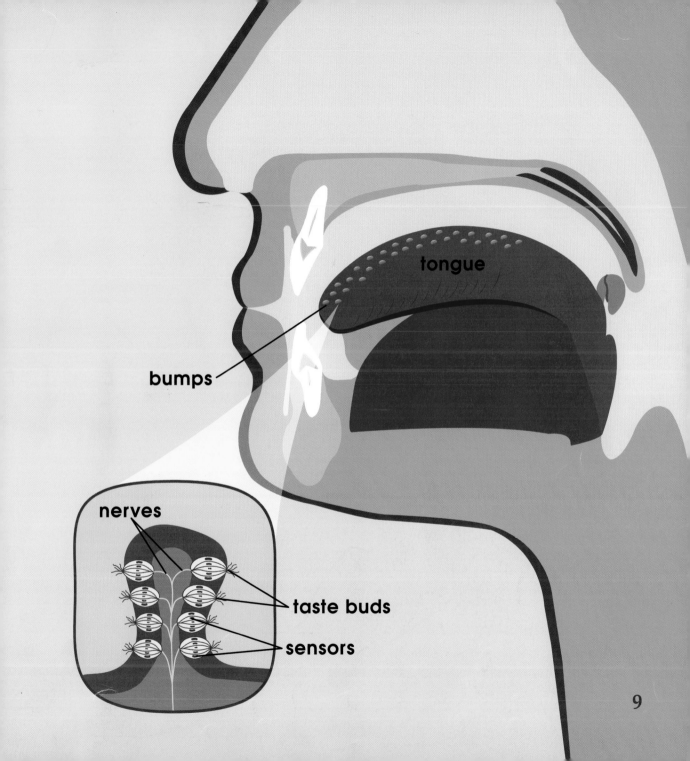

tongue

bumps

nerves

taste buds

sensors

9

salty

bitter

sweet

sour

10

Sensing Different Tastes

Each sensor recognizes a taste. The main tastes are salty, bitter, sweet, and sour. One taste bud can hold sensors for more than one taste.

Some scientists think there is a fifth taste. It is called **umami**. You can taste umami in meat and cheese.

Taste and Smell

The taste buds work with your sense of smell to help you taste flavors. A candy cane would only taste sweet without the sense of smell. But your nose sends a message to your brain about the flavor. Your brain tells you the flavor is mint.

! Fun Fact!

If you couldn't smell, an apple and a potato would taste the same.

Taking Care of Your Mouth

Cleaning your mouth helps protect your sense of taste. Brushing your teeth cleans your whole mouth. Mouthwash helps clean your tongue of germs.

Protect your mouth. Let hot foods cool before eating them. Hot foods can burn your taste buds.

Loss of Taste

The sense of taste weakens as people get older. Taste sensors die. Then new ones grow. As people get older, new sensors don't grow as quickly. A child can usually taste foods better than an adult can.

Butterfly Taste Sensors

The tiny butterfly has an amazing sense of taste. Butterfly tongues are split in two. Each sticky tip has taste buds. Butterflies even have taste sensors on their feet. A butterfly knows if a flower's nectar is good to eat just by stepping on it.

! Fun Fact!
If a butterfly's feet are dipped in sugar water, it will stick out its tongue, looking for food.

Amazing but True!

The giant anteater's tongue is 2 feet (61 centimeters) long. Its long head is shaped to hold its tongue. Ants stick to the tongue's gluey saliva. An anteater sticks its tongue into an anthill 150 times a minute. It can eat 30,000 ants a day.

Hands On: Taste Test

Salty, sour, sweet, and bitter are four main tastes. Do a taste test to see if you can find the tastes on your tongue.

What You Need

pinch of salt
glass of water
few drops of lemon juice
sugar cube or pinch of sugar
small piece of unsweetened
     baking chocolate

What You Do

1. Sprinkle a small pinch of salt on your tongue. Do parts of your tongue taste the saltiness?
2. Drink some water to clear your tongue.
3. Sip some lemon juice. Where do you taste sour?
4. Drink some more water to clear your tongue.
5. Next, let the sugar break down in your mouth. What part of your tongue tastes sweet?
6. Drink more water to clear your tongue.
7. Finally, chew on a tiny piece of baking chocolate. Find the bitter taste on your tongue.

Glossary

crave (KRAVE)—to want something very much

nerve (NURV)—a thin fiber that carries messages between the brain and other parts of the body

saliva (suh-LYE-vuh)—liquid in the mouth that breaks down food

sensor (SEN-sur)—a body part that sends sense messages to nerves

taste buds (TAYST BUDS)—groups of cells in the tongue that sense taste

umami (oo-MAH-mee)—a taste that scientists are studying; umami is a taste found in meat and cheese.

Read More

Cole, Joanna. *The Magic School Bus Explores the Senses.* New York: Scholastic Press, 1999.

Levine, Shar, and Leslie Johnstone. *Super Senses.* First Science Experiments. New York: Sterling Publishing, 2003.

Ziefert, Harriet. *You Can't Taste a Pickle with Your Ear: A Book About Your 5 Senses.* Brooklyn, N.Y.: Blue Apple Books, 2002.

Internet Sites

FactHound offers a safe, fun way to find Internet sites related to this book. All of the sites on FactHound have been researched by our staff.

Here's how:
1. Visit *www.facthound.com*
2. Type in this special code **0736843043** for age-appropriate sites. Or enter a search word related to this book for a more general search.
3. Click on the **Fetch It** button.

FactHound will fetch the best sites for you!

Index